Spot the Differences

Wolverine or Badger?

by Jenna Lee Gleisner

Bullfrog Books

Ideas for Parents and Teachers

Bullfrog Books let children practice reading informational text at the earliest reading levels. Repetition, familiar words, and photo labels support early readers.

Before Reading
- Discuss the cover photo. What does it tell them?
- Look at the picture glossary together. Read and discuss the words.

Read the Book
- "Walk" through the book and look at the photos. Let the child ask questions. Point out the photo labels.
- Read the book to the child, or have them read independently.

After Reading
- Prompt the child to think more. Ask: Have you ever seen a wolverine or badger? Would you like to?

Bullfrog Books are published by Jump!
5357 Penn Avenue South
Minneapolis, MN 55419
www.jumplibrary.com

Copyright © 2025 Jump! International copyright reserved in all countries. No part of this book may be reproduced in any form without written permission from the publisher.

Library of Congress Cataloging-in-Publication Data

Names: Gleisner, Jenna Lee, author.
Title: Wolverine or badger? / by Jenna Lee Gleisner.
Description: Minneapolis, MN: Jump!, Inc., [2025]
Series: Spot the differences | Includes index.
Audience: Ages 5–8
Identifiers: LCCN 2024024834 (print)
LCCN 2024024835 (ebook)
ISBN 9798892136907 (hardcover)
ISBN 9798892136914 (paperback)
ISBN 9798892136921 (ebook)
Subjects: LCSH: Wolverine—Juvenile literature.
American badger—Juvenile literature.
Classification: LCC QL737.C25 G585 2025 (print)
LCC QL737.C25 (ebook)
DDC 599.76/6—dc23/eng/20240621
LC record available at https://lccn.loc.gov/2024024834
LC ebook record available at https://lccn.loc.gov/2024024835

Editor: Katie Chanez
Designer: Emma Almgren-Bersie

Photo Credits: Denja1/iStock, cover (wolverine); Mark Newman/Getty, cover (badger); Roberto Barilani/iStock, 1 (left); Photography by Adri/iStock, 1 (right); AMERICAN BADGER SCRATCHING THE EARTH USA, 3, 14–15; photos martYmage/Shutterstock, 4; Steve Boice/Shutterstock, 5; Medusa's Brother/Shutterstock, 6–7 (top); Dennis Jacobsen/Shutterstock, 6–7 (bottom); AB Photography/iStock, 8–9, 23tr; Geoffrey Kuchera/Shutterstock, 10–11, 23bl, 23br; adamikarl/Shutterstock, 12–13; Hart_Walter/iStock, 15, 23tm; moose henderson/iStock, 16–17; Jen DeVos/Shutterstock, 18–19, 23tl; jamenpercy/iStock, 20; Tony Bosse/Dreamstime, 21; Mikhail Semenov/Shutterstock, 22 (left), 23bm; moosehenderson/Shutterstock, 22 (right); Vladimir Wrangel/Shutterstock, 24 (top); Sean Lema/Shutterstock, 24 (bottom).

Printed in the United States of America at Corporate Graphics in North Mankato, Minnesota.

Table of Contents

Fur and Claws	4
See and Compare	20
Quick Facts	22
Picture Glossary	23
Index	24
To Learn More	24

How to Use This Book

In this book, you will see pictures of both wolverines and badgers. Can you tell which one is in each picture?

Hint: You can find the answers if you flip the book upside down!

Fur and Claws

This is a wolverine.

This is a badger.

They look alike.
But they are different.
How?
Let's see!

Both have fur.
A wolverine is dark.
A badger is light.
Which is this?

Answer: wolverine

A badger has a white stripe.
It has patches.
Where?
On its face.
A wolverine does not.
Which is this?

Answer: badger

Wolverines live by trees.
They climb.
Badgers like open spaces.
Which is this?

Answer: wolverine

Both have claws.
They dig.
Badgers dig in dirt.
Wolverines dig in snow.
Which is this?

claw

Answer: badger

It is winter.

Badgers stay in.

Wolverines go out.

Which is this?

Answer: wolverine

Both hunt.
Badgers wait by burrows.
Wolverines hide.
They pounce.
Which is this?

Answer: badger

See and Compare

Wolverine

- dark fur
- round head
- long tail
- sharp claws
- short legs

Quick Facts

Wolverines and badgers are similar. But they have some differences. Take a look!

Wolverines

- weigh up to 40 pounds (18 kilograms)
- live in areas with mountains and trees
- hunt by hiding and pouncing

Badgers

- weigh about 25 pounds (11 kg)
- live in treeless areas
- hunt by chasing animals into burrows

Picture Glossary

burrows
Tunnels or holes in the ground that animals use as homes.

claws
Hard, sharp nails on an animal's feet.

fur
The coat of thick hair on an animal.

patches
Small areas or spots.

pounce
To jump on something suddenly.

stripe
A thin band of color.

Index

burrows 19
claws 15
climb 13
dig 15
fur 9
hide 19
hunt 19
open spaces 13
patches 10
pounce 19
stripe 10
trees 13

To Learn More

Finding more information is as easy as 1, 2, 3.

❶ Go to www.factsurfer.com

❷ Enter "wolverineorbadger?" into the search box.

❸ Choose your book to see a list of websites.